# Wolf!

"Wolf!" Once upon a time, the
shout would warn shepherds to
keep an eye on their flocks…

THE ANIMAL WORLD

# Written and illustrated by Laura Bour

*Specialist adviser: Dr Jane Mainwaring,*
*The British Museum*
*(Natural History)*

*ISBN 1 85103 035 2*
*First published 1988 in the United Kingdom by*
*Moonlight Publishing Ltd,*
*131 Kensington Church Street, London W8*

*© 1986 by Editions Gallimard*
*Translated by Sarah Matthews*
*English text © 1988 by Moonlight Publishing Ltd*
*Printed in Italy by La Editoriale Libraria*

# Are you scared of meeting a wolf in the woods?

Have you ever been afraid that there might be something fierce, with long fangs and yellow eyes, lurking round the corner waiting to pounce – though you know there's nothing there?

In the Middle Ages, painters drew wolves from their imagination – not from life.

# Why did people fear wolves?

For hundreds of years people thought that wolves were ferocious monsters. They did not understand how wolves lived, and made up stories about them. And it's true that sometimes wolves, if they were very hungry, would creep down near to people's houses, and steal sheep from the fields. They even went right up to the doors and windows if they could smell food.

Sheep were easy prey for a hungry wolf.

# Are they really big, bad wolves?

You may have seen wolves in the zoo, pacing up and down in their cages. But have you ever seen them in the woods? Or on the mountains? Where are they? Even two hundred years ago, wolves were kings of the forest in Europe and North America. Now there are only a few left in Spain, in Poland, Scandinavia, Siberia, China and Tibet, and some in North America. As farming has taken up more land, and woods have been destroyed, wolves have become fewer and fewer. The wolf's worst enemy is man.

The bear and the lynx are
the wolf's only natural enemies.
They too, like the wolf, are now very rare.

1. Wolves, like dogs, mark the limits of their territory with a few drops of urine on landmarks such as stones and bushes.

3. In winter, a pack of five to eight wolves groups together under the leadership of a dominant wolf and his dominant female

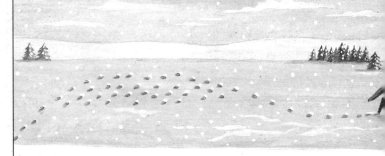

5. Wolves walk in single file, nose to tail, through the snow, leaving only one set of prints.

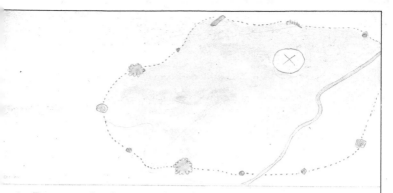

2. Every week, they patrol their territory. It is always large enough to supply all their food, and encloses a stream.

4. They are the two strongest wolves. Only this couple will breed, though all the pack will hunt together to feed the cubs.

6. But when they go round curves, they fan out, and you can tell how many wolves there are in the pack.

## Only the dominant male and female mate.

In spring, they look for a quiet spot where they can raise their young.

Usually they shelter under a rock or a fallen tree, or in a fox's old den.

After nine weeks, the she-wolf gives birth to as many as seven jet-black cubs, which she suckles. As soon as they learn how to walk, the cubs set off exploring. Their mother fetches them back by the scruff of the neck! They like playing and scrapping together until they collapse with tiredness. Bit by bit, the wolf-cubs are taught how to behave in the pack.

The pack members are very patient with the playful, inquisitive cubs.

## <u>Wolves have an extremely varied diet.</u>

In winter wolves eat moose, deer and caribou, prey very much bigger than the wolves themselves. However, in summer, small animals such as beavers, hares, and even mice and frogs make up an important part of the wolves' diet.

When food is short, wolves aren't choosy – they eat snakes, worms, slugs and even grubs. A wolf's stomach can hold up to four kilos of food. They really do wolf everything down!

All the wolves in the pack will chew up meat to feed the cubs.

Trotting upstream, wolves drive the
salmon into shallow pools where they
can be caught with one snap of the
wolves' powerful jaws. Wolves know
how to turn over stones to hunt for
crayfish.
They never kill for pleasure,
only for food.

16

## Hunting in a pack

So that they don't waste energy, wolves test the moose and caribou before launching an attack. They follow about a hundred metres behind, and set the animals running. If one runs quickly, they leave it alone, and keep searching until they find a slower animal, one that is old or ill or wounded.

## Teamwork

The wolves surround their prey and, bit by bit, draw closer together. At last the animal is brought to bay. The wolves leap and the prey is killed quickly by their sharp fangs.

The strongest wolves always eat first while the oldest and the youngest wait their turn, watching avidly.

dominant wolf

submissive wolf

# Wolves can talk to each other
using visual signals. Their whole
bodies show how they feel.

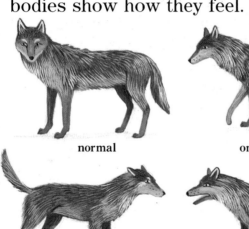

normal

on the alert

threatening

dominant

submissive

completely submissive

**Dogs and wolves have a lot in common.** You know how a dog wags his tail when he's happy, or tucks it between his legs when he's upset – wolves do just the same.

But wolves are faster and stronger than dogs. A wolf's jaw is incredibly powerful – with one bite, it can snap the leg of an adult moose.

Wolves are also very good at running. Over short distances they can run at fifty kilometres an hour, while just jogging along steadily they can travel a hundred kilometres a day.

## A howl in the night

Wolves have all sorts of different cries: growling, snarling, barking, howling. They all mean different things. When they hunt at night, wolves howl to keep in touch with each other and to keep the pack together in the dark.

## A variety of voices

Some wolves have deep voices, some high ones, and some can howl much longer than others. They seem to enjoy howling together at the same time, like singers in a chorus. In the Arctic, Eskimos learnt to understand what the wolves were saying – their cries warned them when game-herds were on their way.

# How did people keep wolves away in times gone by?

When wolves roamed the villages, and even the outskirts of towns, people had to protect their animals and foodstores. They would keep watch, and call out if they saw a wolf (or sometimes, like the little boy who cried wolf, even if they didn't!). Herbs, like wolfsbane, were supposed to keep wolves away. More effective, though, were lights, fires, fences, and things which made a noise to scare the wolves off.

Wolf-light

A carved shape on the end of a rope screeched as it was whirled round.

A vicious pronged pitchfork

A wolf-tile acted as a warning signal: the biting north wind which brought storm and hunger to the wolves, driving them towards the villages, whistled through the holes in the tile, alerting the villagers.

No wolf would attack a dog with spikes like this on its neck.

23

Before they had guns, villagers used to hunt wolves with sturdy dogs and strong sticks.

A wolf-hunt: teams of dogs were needed to keep up with the fast-running wolves. Some dogs, like Irish wolfhounds, were bred specially for this.

The last wild wolf in France was killed in 1977.

Wolf-traps caused terrible pain to wolves caught in them.

# Kill the wolf!

When people lived in small villages, herding sheep and cattle, and often not far off starving themselves, a wolf taking a lamb or a calf could mean disaster. Wolves were the main enemy for these farmers, and they would try any means they could to kill them. They used traps, guns, poison. In England around 1550, a whole forest was burnt down to drive the wolves out. But now, in the countries where wolves still survive, wolf-hunting is carefully controlled or banned altogether.

Hunting wolves from helicopters meant simple slaughter. This kind of massacre is absolutely forbidden now.

# A natural place for a wolf

Every animal has its place in nature. Wolves ate weak and wounded animals, those who were not strong enough to escape. By doing so, they helped to keep the balance of nature, where only the strong survive and breed. Now that they have disappeared from our woods and forests,

wolves have been replaced by
other predators, such as foxes.
As a result, foxes have multiplied and
now they are almost as much of a
plague as wolves were ever thought
to be – particularly as foxes can carry
the killer disease rabies. Farmers
have to kill the foxes. And if the foxes
all died out, then the rabbits and mice
that the foxes eat would begin to
multiply. Farmers would have to hunt
them! The balance of nature is a
delicate thing.

# A wild wolf for a father

Some Eskimos still use dogs to pull their sleds. They need animals which are tough and powerful. So they sometimes do what their forefathers did: they tether a female dog outside the village. A male wolf soon comes and mates with her, and eight weeks later a litter of lively half-wolf puppies is born.

The wolf is most probably the dog's closest ancestor.
The origins of domestic dogs are still unknown.
They may be descended from jackals or from Asian wild dogs, but they probably come from wolves.

Thanks to this mixture, the Eskimos have animals with the size and endurance of wolves and the loyalty of dogs. They regard their Eskimo trainers as their pack-leaders, and obey them just as they would a dominant wolf. But the half-wolves are still very fierce: unless they're well trained they can be a danger to the rest of the team and even to their owners. The training of a wild animal is always tricky, and takes constant care and patience.

# What animals are related to wolves?

'Prairie wolves' or **coyotes** live in North America. They like eating fruit quite as much as rabbits.

On the outskirts of big towns, coyotes love rummaging about in dustbins.

**Jackals** are small, smoother animals. They live on the plains of Africa and America. They hunt at night in family groups.

Jackals don't only scavenge for dead meat – they are good hunters too.

**Cape hunting-dogs,** or painted hyenas, live on the plains of Africa. They take great care of their babies. When they have killed an animal, the cubs are the first to be fed.

Cape hunting-dogs live in groups of up to thirty animals.

The **fennec,** or desert fox, is another cousin of the wolf. It lives in the deserts of Africa and North America. Fennecs are skilful hunters.

**Dingos,** the wild dogs of Australia, arrived there about six thousand years ago, with the last of the Aborigine migrations.

Dingos live and hunt in small packs.

The **Alsatian,** or German shepherd dog, is often said to look like a wolf. Can you see what the differences are?

Alsatians are good guard dogs. They also help mountain rescue teams.

## Some people used to play music to wolves in the forest!

People told stories of magicians leading packs of wolves through the woods to the sound of a wooden pipe, just as the magical Pied Piper of Hamelin led the rats. But these men in the woods weren't really magic, only simple woodcutters or charcoal-burners, people who worked day in, day out in the forest and played the pipe to pass the time. They had learned to make friends with the wolves, which gathered round to hear these two-legged wolves howl almost as well as they could!

Mothers through the ages frightened their children with stories of the Big Bad Wolf who would come and get them if they weren't good.

Romulus, the founder of Rome, and his brother Remus were supposed to have been brought up by a she-wolf.

## Wolf tales

There are hundreds of stories about wolves, from the Wolfman to Rudyard Kipling's Mowgli, from Aesop's *Fables* to *Little Red Riding Hood*.

It's a pity that almost all the stories show wolves as fierce, cunning, cruel and treacherous. Now you know how totally untrue that is.

Werewolves were men who were supposed to turn into wolves at night, especially when there was a full moon. Whoever they bit was said to turn into a werewolf too.

# What will happen to wolves now?

They live protected in zoos, nature reserves and parks.

One traditional story tells how the cunning fox trapped the wolf's tail in ice.

Perhaps one day wolves may be released back into the forests where they used to roam. Before then, though, people must learn to understand them and to respect them and their way of life. Every animal has a right to live its own life, dignified and free. Shall we one day thrill to the sound of wolves howling in the distance on a frosty winter's night?

Little Red Riding Hood

# Index